Your Kookey Stick

Garlic clove

Large shallot

Bouquet garni

Red onion

Nutmeg

Chives

Spring onions

Smoked pancetta

Pitted green olives

Rosemary

Parmesan cheese

Slotted spoon

Baby spinach

Red cherry tomato

Butternut squash

Here are your Kookey Chefs stickers, they will help you identify key items of food when out shopping for your Kookey recipe ingredients.

When asked 'WHAT'S THIS?' find the correct sticker, peel-off and place within the dotty lines.

Cook Pasta with Paulie

CONTENTS

Meet Paulie

Hi, my name is Paulie

I am one of the Kookey Chefs. We are a team of cheeky little monsters who just love to cook and create a storm in the kitchen. We used to live in the kitchen cupboards amongst all our favourite things and only came out when no adults were around, until one day our cover was blown and we were found. But now our secret is out, the Kookey Chefs and I would love to share all our knowledge with you and help you become a better chef!

Io Amo la Pasta! this means 'I Love Pasta' and I simply do. There is so much you can do with it. You can eat it hot or cold, at lunch or dinner and it goes with almost everything!

Before you start get an adult to help you and from now on you are a Kookey Chef apprentice! Have fun.

Love Paulie X

PAULIE
Pasta Chef

Age: 12
Favourite Food: PASTA
Kitchen Tool: SLOTTED SPOON
Love: ITALIAN FOOD

BEFORE YOU BEGIN PLEASE...PLEASE...PLEASE READ OUR KOOKEY CHEF RULES... IT IS VERY IMPORTANT THAT EVERY KOOKEY CHEF FOLLOWS THEM CLOSELY

WHAT'S THIS?

Kookey Kitchen Rules

Cooking is fun but hot cookers and sharp knives can also make it very dangerous. Follow these simple rules whenever you decide to cook and also have an adult around to help at all times.

1. Be careful!
Never cook anything unless there is an adult there to help you.

2. What to wear
Always roll your sleeves up and tie back any long hair. Don't have anything loose that could catch fire. Always wear an apron.

3. Weighing and measuring
Always use weighing scales, measuring spoons and measuring jugs when weighing out your ingredients.

4. Using the cooker
Always ask an adult to turn the oven on for you. Some recipes will ask you to preheat the oven, which means turn the oven on before you start cooking. Never open the oven door when cooking and always ask an adult to put in and take out your food from the oven. And don't forget to turn it off.

5. Chopping and slicing
Always ask an adult to help you cut your ingredients. Be very careful with sharp knives. Hold them with the blade pointing downwards and always use a chopping board. Keep your fingers away from the blades and tip. Sometimes it may be easier to chop vegetables with a pair of scissors.

6. Stirring
When you are stirring food in a saucepan, always hold the pan firmly by the handle. If you need to stir something on the hob always ask an adult for help.

7. Hot things
Always clear a space ready for hot things. Wear oven gloves or get an adult to help you and place straight onto a wooden board or heat stand. Never put directly onto the work surface.

8. Using the hob
Always get an adult to help you when cooking on the hob. Make sure you turn saucepan handles to the side so you do not knock them.

9. Washing up
Always wash up as you go along. Keep a cloth nearby so that you can wipe up any spills immediately.

10. Dry hands
Always make sure your hands are dry before you plug in or disconnect an electric gadget such as an electric hand whisk. Ask an adult for help when using these kitchen tools.

Hygiene Rules

1. Wash all fruit and vegetables before cooking or eating.
2. Always use separate chopping boards for meat and vegetables.
3. Don't spread germs — always wash your hands before and after cooking especially after touching raw meat or fish.
4. Store cooked and raw food separately.
5. Keep meat and fish in the fridge until needed and ensure they are cooked properly.
6. Always check the 'use by' dates on all ingredients. Never use out of date food.

DID YOU KNOW? The longest strand of pasta measured 3,776 metres!!

All About Pasta

For hundreds of years pasta has been popular in Italy, but it is now eaten all over the world. There are so many different types of pasta from long or short, to thick and thin.

So what's pasta made of?

Most pasta is made with special durum wheat flour and water, but often has eggs added to the mixture to make a delicious rich pasta. So check the packet and see whether it contains the word "all'uovo" or "with egg". There is even different coloured pasta to choose from. Green pasta is made with spinach, red pasta with tomatoes or red peppers and the black pasta is made from squid ink!

Types of dried pasta

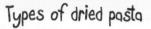

1. **Long wide and thin pasta** choose from pasta such as pappardelle which is wide and long (top left) or tagliatelle which is often sold in nests and is thinner than pappardelle (bottom left). The thinner long pastas are spaghetti (far right) and linguine (middle) which is like flat spaghetti. All are great for oily sauces.

2. **Short ridged pasta** small but chunky tubes of pasta covered in ridges are ideal for thick sauces. Look out for rigatoni (left) or penne that has been cut on the diagonal (right).

3. **Shaped pasta** available in so many shapes and sizes. All are good for sauces as they sit in the curves of the shapes. Why not try conchiglie shaped like small shells (top) or farfalle, the bows (right). Orrecchiette is known as 'little ears' (top left) and macaroni which are small thin tubes great for combining with a cheesy sauce and baking in the oven (bottom).

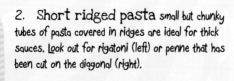

4. **Baking pasta** some pasta is great for combining with chunky sauces and baking in the oven topped with lots of cheese. Cannelloni are smooth tubes of pasta perfect for stuffing with creamy fillings, or why not choose lasagne sheets. These flat sheets are ideal for layering chunky sauces and baking in the oven.

5. **Spiral pasta** this pasta opens out like a corkscrew when cooking and is great for clingy sauces. Choose from fusilli (top), trottole (right) or bucati fusilli (left).

6. **Tiny pasta** mini pastas are great for adding to soups and salads. Orzo is so small it almost looks like rice and these tiny pasta grains give a wonderful creamy texture to any dish.

Why not use wholewheat pasta instead which is bursting with goodness and helps keep you fuller for longer?

Pasta should be cooked until it is 'al dente', which in Italian means 'to the tooth'. It describes the texture of the food when it is properly cooked but just firm to the bite

Paulie's fact phone... COOKING PASTA

The cooking time of pasta depends on the type of pasta you are using and it's shape. Fresh pasta and long thin shapes will cook more quickly than chunky shapes, so always check the instructions on the packet before cooking for the most accurate cooking time.

1. Fill a very large saucepan with water it should be about three-quarters full. Turn on the heat and bring the water to the boil.

2. When the water is boiling continuously, add a teaspoon of salt and a tablespoon of oil (this stops it from sticking together). Using a slotted spoon, carefully lower the pasta into the water and stir to separate it. The water will immediately stop boiling for a minute or so, as soon as it comes back to the boil start the cooking time according to the instructions on the packet. Stir from time to time to prevent the pasta from clumping together.

3. Once the pasta has cooked for the correct time, it should be 'al dente'. Pasta should never be overcooked, it should be firm and tender, but not soggy.

4. To drain the pasta, stand the colander in the sink and pour the pasta into it. If the pasta needs to wait while you finish off the sauce, pour about a teaspoon of oil over it in the colander and toss to coat, this stops the pasta from sticking together.

REMEMBER...

1. Thin and long pasta is best for oily and runny sauces
2. Wide and shaped pasta is perfect for chunky and thick sauces

How To Use The Recipes

There's loads of information packed into every page. Use the key below as a way of finding your way around the recipes and remember to look out for Paulie, he'll give you hints and tips along the way.

Shopping list

Recipe info or 'splat level'

What to do next and when to do it

Pea and Bacon Squiggles

SERVES **4** TAKES **20** MINUTES DIFFICULTY RATING **2**

You will need...

- 1 garlic clove
- 40g Parmesan cheese
- 100g frozen petit pois or peas
- 350g dried fusilli bucati pasta
- 1 tbsp olive oil
- 1 x 180g pack smoked bacon lardons
- 4 tbsp double cream

WHAT'S THIS?

Prepare... 1
On a chopping board, peel the garlic clove and crush with the garlic press. Grate the Parmesan cheese and put the peas in a small bowl.

Cook the Pasta... 2
Bring a saucepan of water to the boil. Add the pasta with a slotted spoon and cook for 10-12 minutes or follow the pack instructions, stirring occasionally. Drain the pasta in a colander.

Make the Sauce... 3
Add the oil to the wide shallow pan and heat gently for 30 seconds. Add the lardons and cook for 2-3 minutes until just brown. Add the garlic and peas and cook for a further 2 minutes to heat through.

Mix it... 4
Add the pasta to the pan with the bacon, garlic and bean mixture. Stir in the cream, grated Parmesan and 1 tbsp hot water. Stir over a gentle heat until the cheese has melted.

5
...Season with black pepper and serve immediately

Bacon lardons are small pieces of thick cut bacon sold ready chopped

Things I need to remember!

If you can't find fusilli bucati then just use normal fusilli.

8   9

Your Kookey Sticker dotty line

Paulie 'know how'

Your Kookey note pad

Paulie tip

Always collect all the ingredients before you start any cooking. Then weigh and measure the ingredients accurately, checking the recipe as you do to make sure you have everything you need.

When a recipe tells you how long to cook something for, set a timer that way you won't overcook or burn your food

6

Pea and Bacon Squiggles

SERVES **4** TAKES **20** MINUTES DIFFICULTY RATING **2**

You will need...

- 1 garlic clove
- 40g Parmesan cheese
- 100g frozen petit pois or peas
- 350g dried fusilli bucati pasta
- 1 tbsp olive oil
- 1 x 180g pack smoked bacon lardons
- 4 tbsp double cream

→ WHAT'S THIS?

Bacon lardons are small pieces of thick cut bacon sold ready chopped

1

Prepare...

On a chopping board, peel the garlic clove and crush with the garlic press. Grate the Parmesan cheese and put the peas in a small bowl.

2

Cook the pasta...

Bring a saucepan of water to the boil. Add the pasta with a slotted spoon and cook for 10-12 minutes or follow the pack instructions, stirring occasionally. Drain the pasta in a colander.

3

Make the sauce...

Add the oil to a wide shallow pan and heat gently for 30 seconds. Add the lardons and cook for 2-3 minutes until just brown. Add the garlic and peas and cook for a further 2 minutes stirring to heat through.

Kookey Kitchen Tools

Here are all the kitchen utensils you will need to follow the recipes in this book. Check that you have the right tools before starting the recipes.

1. Slotted spoon
2. Ladle
3. Whisk
4. Can opener
5. Wooden spoon
6. Spatula
7. Scissors
8. Vegetable peeler
9. Measuring spoons
10. Tongs
11. Wide shallow pan

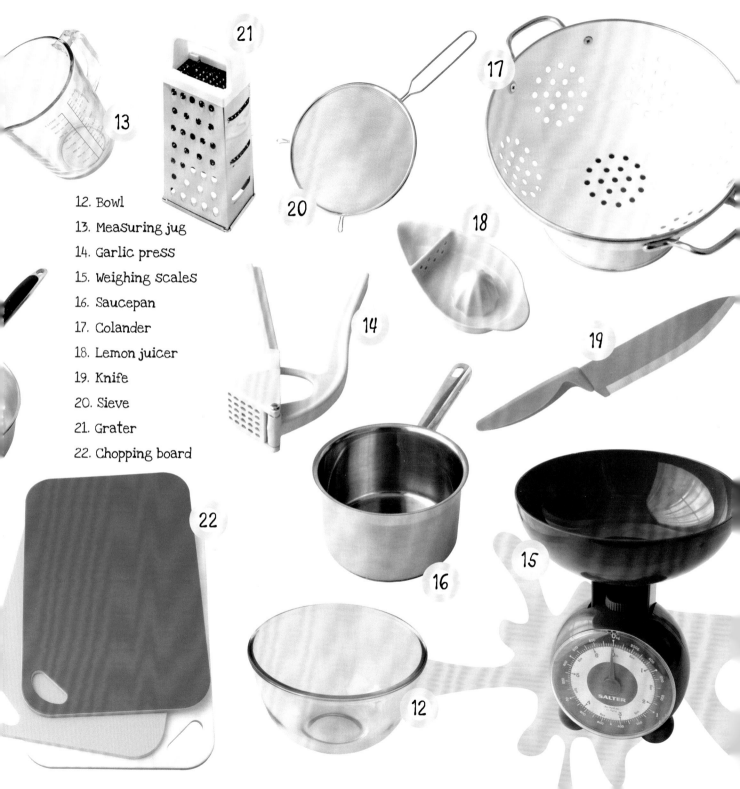

12. Bowl
13. Measuring jug
14. Garlic press
15. Weighing scales
16. Saucepan
17. Colander
18. Lemon juicer
19. Knife
20. Sieve
21. Grater
22. Chopping board

Open out this page
and take a look at your
Kookey Kitchen Tools.

In order for you to proceed with
the following Kookey recipes
more easily, you'll need to
ensure you have them in your
Kookey Kitchen.

open here

Mix it...

Add the pasta to the pan with the bacon, garlic and pea mixture. Stir in the cream, grated Parmesan and 1 tbsp hot water. Stir over a gentle heat until the cheese has melted.

Things I need to remember!

...Season with black pepper and serve immediately.

If you can't find fusilli bucati then just use normal fusilli

9

Traffic Light Chicken Salad

SERVES **4**   TAKES **30** MINUTES   DIFFICULTY RATING **1**

You will need...

- 150g skinless cooked chicken
- 12 red cherry tomatoes
- 1/4 red onion
- 10g fresh coriander
- 1/2 green pepper
- 1/2 yellow pepper
- 250g dried conchiglie pasta
- 1-2 tsp mild curry paste
- 2 tbsp lemon juice
- 4 tbsp reduced fat mayonnaise
- 2 tbsp Greek yoghurt

WHAT'S THIS?

1

Prepare...

Put the chicken on a chopping board and tear into small pieces. Put the cherry tomatoes on another chopping board and cut in half. Peel, trim the ends and finely chop the onion. Remove the leaves from the coriander and chop. Cut the sides off the pepper, remove the seeds and finely chop the flesh.

2

Cook the pasta...

Bring a saucepan of water to the boil. Add the pasta with a slotted spoon and cook for 10-12 minutes or following the pack, stirring occasionally. Drain the pasta in a colander and rinse in cold water. Drain again thoroughly.

3

Mix it...

Meanwhile put the chicken, tomatoes, onion, coriander, both peppers, curry paste, lemon juice, mayonnaise and yoghurt into a large bowl. Add the cooked pasta and mix together.

4

...Serve immediately.

Things I need to remember!

This makes a perfect lunchbox treat, simply store in an airtight container ready for lunchtime

Salmon and Broccoli Trottole

SERVES **4**   TAKES **45** MINUTES   DIFFICULTY RATING **5**

You will need...

- 4 spring onions
- 150g tenderstem broccoli
- 1 tbsp freshly chopped dill (optional)
- 300g skinless salmon fillet
- 1 bay leaf
- 6 peppercorns
- 300ml semi-skimmed milk
- 25g butter
- 1 tbsp plain flour
- 2 tsp wholegrain mustard
- 150g crème fraiche
- 2 tsp lemon juice
- 300g dried trottole pasta

WHAT'S THIS?

1

Prepare...

Put the spring onions on a chopping board, trim the ends and slice diagonally. Trim the broccoli heads into small pieces and finely slice the stems. Chop the dill.

2

Cook the salmon...

Put the salmon in a wide shallow pan with the bay leaf, peppercorns and milk. Put over a gentle heat, bring to a simmer, cover with a lid and simmer for 2 minutes. Then remove from the heat for 10 minutes to cool. Remove the salmon from the milk with a slotted spoon (don't throw the milk away) and put on a plate. Use a fork to separate the flesh into large flakes.

3

Make the sauce...

Pour the reserved milk through a sieve into a jug. Melt the butter in a saucepan over a gentle heat, add the spring onions and cook gently for 1-2 minutes. Add the flour and cook for another minute. Remove from the heat and slowly add the reserved milk, stirring constantly until smooth. Return to the heat and simmer for 1-2 minutes, stirring until thickened. Stir in the mustard, dill, crème fraiche and lemon juice. Season with a pinch of salt and pepper.

4

Cook the pasta and broccoli...

Bring a saucepan of water to the boil. Add the pasta with a slotted spoon and cook for 8-9 minutes following the pack instructions, stirring occasionally. Add the broccoli heads and stems for the last 3-5 minutes. Drain in a colander and return to the pan.

5

Mix it...

Warm the sauce through over a gentle heat, gradually stir in the salmon and then add the pasta and broccoli, mix well together.

6

...Serve immediately.

Things I need to remember!

Spicy Sausage Ragu

SERVES **4**   TAKES **40** MINUTES   DIFFICULTY RATING **2**

You will need...

- ½ red onion
- 1 garlic clove
- 100g cherry tomatoes
- 4 x good quality large herby sausages
- 100g marinated antipasti peppers
- 1 tbsp olive oil
- 1/4 tsp crushed chilli flakes
- 1 tsp dried oregano
- 300ml passata
- 2 tsp Worcestershire sauce
- 300g dried penne pasta

WHAT'S THIS?

1

Prepare...

On a chopping board, peel, trim the ends and finely chop the onion. Peel and crush the garlic with the garlic press. Halve the cherry tomatoes. Put the sausages on another board. Using scissors, snip the sausages in half then squeeze the sausagemeat out from their skins and break up into even sized chunks. Drain the peppers in a sieve over a bowl.

Antipasti peppers are Italian peppers marinated in oil

2

Make the sauce...

Put the oil in a wide shallow pan and heat gently for 30 seconds. Add the onion and garlic and cook for 2-3 minutes. Turn up the heat, add the sausagemeat and cook for a further 5-6 minutes until lightly browned, stirring occasionally. Add the chilli flakes, cherry tomatoes, oregano, passata, peppers, Worcestershire sauce and 100ml water and stir well together. Bring to a simmer, put the lid on and cook for a further 5 minutes. If needed, add salt and pepper to taste.

14

Cook the pasta...

Meanwhile, bring a saucepan of water to the boil. Add the pasta with a slotted spoon and cook for 10-12 minutes or following the pack, stirring occasionally. Drain the pasta in a colander then spoon into the ragu sauce.

Things I need to remember!

...Stir to coat and serve immediately.

Try using spicy Spanish chorizo sausages instead, or if you don't like it spicy at all, leave out the chilli flakes

Cheesy Pesto Bows

SERVES  **4**   TAKES **25** MINUTES   DIFFICULTY RATING **3**

You will need...

- 2 x 25g packs fresh basil
- 2 garlic cloves
- 1 tbsp pine nuts
- 6 tbsp olive oil
- 400g dried farfalle pasta
- 25g Parmesan cheese

You could try adding other herbs such as parsley or chives, or replace the basil with wild rocket instead for a peppery pesto

WHAT'S THIS?

1
Prepare...

Put the basil on a chopping board and strip the leaves from the stalks. Peel and chop the garlic and finely grate the Parmesan.

2
Make the pesto...

Put the basil, garlic, pine nuts and oil in the food processor and whiz to a coarse paste. Use the spatula to push the paste back down into the bowl and whiz again. Scrape the pesto out into a bowl and stir in the Parmesan.

3
Cook the pasta...

Bring a saucepan of water to the boil. Add the pasta with a slotted spoon and cook for 11-13 minutes or following the pack instructions, stirring occasionally. Drain the pasta in a colander.

16

Mix it...

4

Return the pasta to the pan and stir in the pesto with a wooden spoon until evenly coated.

Things I need to remember!

5

...Spoon into bowls and serve immediatley.

Hearty Minestrone

SERVES **4**   TAKES **1** HOUR   DIFFICULTY RATING **3**

You will need...

- 1 large shallot
- 1 garlic clove
- 1 tbsp rosemary leaves
- 2 rashers smoked streaky bacon
- 1 carrot
- 2 baby leeks
- 1 celery stick
- 30g french beans
- 1 tbsp olive oil
- 2 tbsp sun dried tomato paste
- 1.5 ltr good vegetable stock
- 100g dried linguine pasta

WHAT'S THIS?

1

Prepare...

Put the shallot on a chopping board, peel, trim the ends and finely chop. Peel the garlic clove and crush with a garlic press. Finely chop the rosemary. Using scissors, cut the bacon into small pieces. Peel and finely chop the carrot. Trim the leeks, celery and beans and finely chop.

2

Cook the vegetables...

Put the oil into a large pan and heat gently for 30 seconds. Add the shallot, garlic and rosemary and cook for 2 minutes. Add the bacon and cook for a further 2 minutes until starting to brown. Add the carrot, leeks and celery and cook for another 3 minutes. Stir in the tomato paste, then add the stock, cover and simmer for about 10 minutes.

Use tiny pasta shapes such as Farfallini, Conchigletti or Fusellini

18

3

Cook the pasta...

Break up the linguine into about 3cm pieces and add to the soup with the beans. Return to the boil, cover and simmer again for another 8-10 minutes or until the pasta is cooked and the vegetables are tender, season.

Things I need to remember!

4

...Ladle into mugs and serve immediately.

Three Cheese Macaroni

SERVES 6   TAKES 45 MINUTES   DIFFICULTY RATING 4

You will need...

- 1 x 400g can cherry tomatoes
- 75g Gruyere cheese
- 50g Parmesan cheese
- 450ml semi skimmed milk
- pinch freshly grated nutmeg
- 75g ciabatta bread
- 300g dried macaroni pasta
- 75g butter, plus extra for greasing
- 50g plain flour
- 2 tsp mustard powder
- 125g mascarpone cheese
- 1 x 80g bag baby spinach leaves

WHAT'S THIS?

1

Prepare...

Preheat the oven to Gas 5/190C/fan 170C. Grease a large ovenproof dish. Tip the tomatoes into a sieve over a bowl and set aside to drain. Grate the Gruyere and Parmesan cheeses on a chopping board. Grate the nutmeg. Tear the ciabatta into pieces and coarsely grate to make rough breadcrumbs.

2

Cook the pasta...

Bring a saucepan of water to the boil. Add the pasta with a slotted spoon and cook for 10-12 minutes or following the pack, stirring occasionally. Drain the pasta in a colander. Return to the pan.

3

Make the sauce...

Meanwhile, melt 50g butter in a pan over a gentle heat, stir in the flour and mustard powder and cook for 1 minute. Remove from the heat and gradually add the milk, stirring until smooth. Return to the heat, stirring constantly until it thickens and reaches the boil, about 5-6 minutes. Add the Gruyere, Parmesan, mascarpone and nutmeg and mix well to melt the cheeses. Season with black pepper if needed.

Mix it...

Add the cheese sauce to the pasta and gradually stir in the spinach and drained tomatoes. Spoon into the prepared dish. Melt the remaining butter in a small pan and stir in the ciabatta crumbs. Spoon the crumbs over the macaroni and put in the oven for 10-15 minutes until bubbling and golden on top.

Things I need to remember!

...Serve immediately.

You don't need to add salt as the Parmesan and Gruyere are already salty

Warm Deli Pasta

SERVES **4** TAKES **25** MINUTES DIFFICULTY RATING **1**

You will need...

- 80g Italian salami slices
- 1 x 150g bag mozzarella
- 1 garlic clove
- 1/2 x 25g pack flat-leaf parsley
- 300g dried fusilli pasta
- 5 tbsp olive oil
- 2 tbsp white wine vinegar
- 2 tsp Dijon mustard
- ½ tsp runny honey
- 75g pitted green olives
- 100g sunblush tomatoes

WHAT'S THIS?

1 Prepare...

On a chopping board using scissors cut the salami into strips. On another chopping board peel and crush the garlic with the garlic press and roughly chop the parsley. Drain the liquid from the mozzarella and tear into rough pieces.

2 Cook the pasta...

Bring a saucepan of water to the boil. Add the pasta with a slotted spoon and cook for 9-11 minutes or following the pack instructions, stirring occasionally. Drain the pasta in a colander and return to the pan.

3 Make the vinaigrette...

Meanwhile, put the olive oil, white wine vinegar, mustard, honey, garlic and parsley into a jam jar. Screw the lid on tightly and shake vigorously.

22

4

Mix it...

Pour the dressing immediately over the warm pasta in the pan and stir to coat with the wooden spoon. Add the salami, mozzarella, olives and tomatoes. Return to the heat and stir until the mozzarella starts to melt.

Things I need to remember!

5

...Serve immediately.

Sunblushed tomatoes are tomatoes which have been gently roasted then usually marinated in oregano, garlic and olive oil

Tommy Chicken Rigatoni

You will need...

- 1 small onion
- 1 garlic clove
- 400 g skinless chicken breast fillets
- 1 tbsp olive oil
- 2 tbsp tomato puree
- 1 vegetable stock cube
- 1 bouquet garni
- 1 tbsp balsamic vinegar
- 1 tbsp tomato ketchup
- 1 tsp caster sugar
- 1 x 400 g can chopped tomatoes
- 300g dried rigatoni pasta
- a handful of fresh basil leaves

WHAT'S THIS?

1

Prepare...

Put the onion on a chopping board and cut in half. Peel the brown skin, trim the ends and finely chop. Peel the garlic clove and crush using the garlic press. Put the chicken fillets on another chopping board and cut into small cubes.

2

Make the sauce...

Put the olive oil in a wide shallow pan and heat gently for 30 seconds. Add the onion and garlic and cook for 2-3 minutes until starting to soften. Stir in the tomato puree and cook for 1 minute. Crumble in the stock cube, then add the bouquet garni, balsamic vinegar, ketchup, sugar, tomatoes and 125ml water. Bring to the boil and simmer for 5 minutes.

3

Cook the chicken...

Add the chicken to the pan, cover with a lid and cook for 6-8 minutes until the chicken is cooked through, stirring occasionally.

4

Cook the pasta...

Meanwhile, bring a saucepan of water to the boil. Add the pasta and cook for 10-12 minutes or following the pack instructions. Carefully drain in a colander.

5

Mix it...

Remove the bouquet garni from the sauce using a slotted spoon and season. Add the pasta to the sauce and mix well together.

Things I need to remember!

6

...Serve immediately in bowls and scatter with the basil.

A bouquet garni is a mix of dried or fresh herbs used to flavour soups, casseroles and sauces and is removed after cooking

Tortelloni Soup

SERVES **4**   TAKES **30** MINUTES   DIFFICULTY RATING **1**

You will need...

- 1 carrot
- 4 spring onions
- 1 sprig fresh flat-leaf parsley
- 2 tbsp grated Parmesan
- 15g butter
- 50g frozen peas
- 50g frozen sweetcorn
- 1 ltr good chicken stock
- 1 x 300g pack fresh Chicken and Bacon Tortellini

WHAT'S THIS?

1

Prepare...

Put the spring onions on a chopping board, trim and finely slice. Peel, trim and finely chop the carrot. Roughly chop the parsley and measure the Parmesan.

2

Cook the vegetables...

Put the butter in a large pan and heat gently until melted. Add the carrot and cook for 8-10 minutes until beginning to soften. Add the spring onions and cook for another 2 minutes. Add the frozen peas, sweetcorn and stock and bring to the boil.

26

Cook the Pasta...

Add the tortellini with a slotted spoon and cook for 3-4 minutes or following the pack instructions. Stir in the parsley and season. Ladle the soup into bowls.

Things I need to remember!

4

...Serve immediately with grated Parmesan.

There is a huge choice of filled pastas now on the supermarket shelves, use whatever you like for this recipe

Easy Peasy Spag Bol

SERVES 4   **TAKES** 1½ **HOURS**   **DIFFICULTY RATING** 3

You will need...

- ½ onion
- 1 small carrot
- 1 celery stick
- 2 garlic cloves
- ½ x 110g packet smoked pancetta
- 1 tbsp olive oil
- 1 x 500g pack beef mince
- 1 x 400g can chopped tomatoes
- 3 tbsp sun-dried tomato paste
- 1 large bay leaf
- 300ml good beef stock
- 300g dried spaghetti

> WHAT'S THIS?

1 Prepare...

On a chopping board peel the onion, trim the ends and chop finely. Peel the carrot, trim the ends and finely dice. Trim the celery and chop finely. Peel the garlic cloves and crush using the garlic press. On another chopping board snip the pancetta with scissors into equal sized pieces.

2 Start the sauce...

Add the oil to a wide shallow pan and heat gently for 30 seconds. Add the onion, carrot, celery, garlic and pancetta and cook gently for about 8-10 minutes until softened and just beginning to brown. Stir ocassionly to separate the pancetta with a wooden spoon.

3 Add the meat...

Turn the heat up, add the beef mince and cook for about 5 minutes until browned, stirring to break up the lumps with the wooden spoon.

4 Finish the sauce...

Add the tomatoes, sun-dried tomato paste, bay leaf and stock and bring to the boil. Reduce the heat to a gentle simmer, put the lid on and cook for about 1 hour, stirring from time to time. Keep checking the sauce, if too dry add a little water from a warm kettle.

5

Cook the pasta...

After the sauce has cooked for 45 minutes bring a saucepan of water to the boil. Add the pasta with a slotted spoon and push down. Cook for 5-7 minutes or following the pack instructions, stirring occasionally. Drain the pasta in a colander. Then using a spaghetti spoon or tongs to transfer to the meat pan and gently toss to cover in the sauce.

Things I need to remember!

...Serve immediately.

You can always use streaky bacon instead of pancetta if preferred

Jewel Tuna Salad

You will need...

- 1/4 cucumber
- 1 x 198g can sweetcorn
- 1 x 185g can tuna chunks in brine
- 1/2 red pepper
- 2 tbsp snipped chives
- 3 tbsp mayonnaise
- juice 1/2 small lemon
- 350g dried orrecchiette pasta

WHAT'S THIS?

1

Prepare...

Put the cucumber on a chopping board and cut in half, remove the seeds with a teaspoon and finely dice. Tip the sweetcorn and tuna into a sieve over a bowl, set aside to drain. Remove the seeds from the pepper and finely chop the flesh. Snip the chives with scissors.

2

Cook the pasta...

Bring a saucepan of water to the boil. Add the pasta with a slotted spoon and cook for 11-13 minutes following the pack instructions, stirring occasionally. Drain the pasta in a colander and rinse in cold water drain again thoroughly.

3

Mix it...

Put the cucumber, sweetcorn, tuna, red pepper, chives, mayonnaise and lemon juice into a large bowl. Add the pasta and stir together until combined with a wooden spoon.

...Season and serve.

If you can't find orrecchiette, Rotelline (little wheels) would also work well

Things I need to remember!

31

Creamy Popeye Cannelloni

SERVES **4**   TAKES **1¼** HOURS   DIFFICULTY RATING **4**

You will need...

- 1/2 onion
- 1 x 100g bag baby spinach
- 75g Parmesan cheese
- 100g mozzarella
- 1 egg yolk, lightly beaten
- 25g butter plus extra for greasing
- 1 x 150g pack Boursin cheese
- 8 dried Canelloni tubes
- 500ml passata
- 1 tbsp fresh oregano (optional)

WHAT'S THIS?

1

Prepare...

Preheat the oven to Gas 2/200C/Fan 180C. Grease a large ovenproof dish. Put the onion on a chopping board, peel, trim the ends and finely chop. Roughly chop the spinach, discarding any large stalks. Finely grate the Parmesan and coarsely grate the mozzarella. Place the yolk in a small bowl and beat lightly with a fork.

2

Make the filling...

Put the butter in a pan and heat gently until melted, add the onion and cook for 3-4 minutes until softened. Turn up the heat and add the spinach, cook for 4 minutes until wilted and the moisture has evaporated. Set aside to cool for 10 minutes.

3

Assemble...

Put the Boursin cheese in a medium bowl with two-thirds of the Parmesan and the egg yolk. Add the spinach mixture and stir well. Season. With a teaspoon carefully push the spinach mixture into each cannelloni tube until it is all used up.

4

Bake...

Pour about a third of the passata into the dish, swirling to cover the base and lay the cannelloni tubes on top in a neat row. Pour the remaining passata over the cannelloni, making sure the tubes are well covered, sprinkle with the mozzarella and remaining Parmesan. Bake for 30-35 minutes until golden brown and bubbling.

Things I need to remember!

...Scatter over oregano and serve.

Passata is a smooth sauce made from sieving tomatoes

Herby Meatballs

SERVES 4 TAKES 1½ HOURS DIFFICULTY RATING 5

You will need...

- 50g medium sliced brown bread
- 3 garlic cloves
- 1 red onion
- ½ small lemon
- 1 tbsp fresh rosemary leaves
- 250g pork mince
- 250g beef mince
- 1 tsp Dijon mustard
- 1 egg yolk
- 3 tbsp olive oil
- 2 x 400g cans chopped tomatoes
- 3 tbsp tomato ketchup
- 2 tsp caster sugar
- 300g dried tagliatelle pasta

WHAT'S THIS?

1
Prepare...

On a chopping board grate the bread into coarse crumbs. Peel and crush the garlic cloves using the garlic press. Peel, trim the ends from the onion and finely chop. Grate the zest from the lemon using the grater. Finely chop the rosemary.

Make the meatballs...

Put the breadcrumbs, a third of the garlic, half the chopped onion, pork and beef mince, mustard, lemon zest, rosemary and egg yolk into a bowl and mix together. Using clean hands, shape the mixture into 20 equal sized balls and place on a plate. Cover with cling film and chill for 30 minutes.

3
Cook the meatballs...

Put 1 tbsp of oil in the wide shallow pan and heat gently for 30 seconds. Add 10 meatballs using the tongs and cook gently for 5-6 minutes, turning from time to time until evenly browned. Remove from the pan and put onto a plate. Cook the remaining 10 meatballs in the same way with another 1 tbsp oil. Transfer to the plate.

4
Make the sauce...

Put the remaining oil into the meatball pan and heat gently for 30 seconds. Add the remaining garlic and onion and cook for 2-3 minutes until beginning to soften. Add the tomatoes, ketchup, sugar 3 tbsp cold water and return the meatballs. Bring to a simmer and cook gently for 10 minutes until thickened slightly and meatballs are cooked.

5

Cook the pasta...

Meanwhile bring a saucepan of water to the boil. Add the pasta with a slotted spoon and cook for 10-11 minutes or following the pack instructions, stirring occasionally. Drain the pasta in a colander. Divide the pasta between bowls and top with the meatballs and sauce.

Things I need to remember!

6

...Serve immediately.

Why not try other long pastas, such as Papparadelle, Fusilli Lunghi or Tripoline?

Squash Ham and Mushroom Orzo

SERVES **4**   TAKES **45** MINUTES   DIFFICULTY RATING **3**

You will need...

- 1/2 onion
- 500g butternut squash
- 1 garlic clove
- 1 x 150g packet button mushrooms
- 75g sliced smoked ham
- 6 large sage leaves
- 25g butter
- 75g grated Emmental or Gruyere cheese
- 100ml single cream
- 300g dried orzo pasta

WHAT'S THIS?

1

Prepare...

On a chopping board, peel the onion, trim the ends and finely chop. Peel the butternut squash and cut into small cubes. Peel the garlic and crush with the garlic press. Wipe the mushrooms with a damp piece of kitchen towel, trim the stalks and halve. Using scissors, cut the ham into strips. Roll the sage leaves into a bundle and finely slice.

2

Cook the vegetables...

Put the butter in a wide pan over a gentle heat until melted, add the onion and squash. Cover with a lid and cook for 8-10 minutes, stirring from time to time. Add the garlic and mushrooms, cover again and cook for a further 10-12 minutes or until the squash is tender when pierced with a skewer. Stir in the ham and sage and cook for a further minute.

3

Cook the pasta...

Meanwhile, bring a saucepan of water to the boil. Add the pasta with a slotted spoon and cook for 7-8 minutes or following the pack instructions, stirring occasionally. Drain the pasta in a colander.

4

Mix it...

Add the pasta to the squash, ham and mushroom mixture, then add the cheese and cream, stir well together.

Things I need to remember!

5

...Season and serve immediately.

As a short cut, look out for bags of ready prepared squash in the supermarkets

Glossary

If you don't know what a word means, look it up here!

AB

BOIL to heat a liquid until lots of large bubbles break the surface

BROWN or GOLDEN to cook food, usually by baking, frying or grilling so that it becomes light brown in colour

C

CHILL to put into the fridge

CHOP to cut food into either small or large pieces

CONSISTENCY how thick or thin something is

COARSE PASTE to mix ingredients together in a food processor or blender until it has a rough texture but is spreadable

D

DESEED to remove the seeds

DICE to cut the ingredient into small even sized pieces

DISSOLVE to melt a solid into a liquid usually with heat

DRAIN to use a colander or sieve to remove the liquid

EFG

GOLDEN or BROWN to cook food, usually by baking, frying or grilling so that it becomes light brown in colour

GRATE to use a grater to make strands of food. Use large grater holes for coarsely grating and the small holes for finely grating

GREASE or GREASING to apply a thin layer of fat such as oil or butter to a dish or tray to stop it from sticking

HIJK

HEAT to put pan on the hob and turn on to increase the temperature of the ingredients

INGREDIENTS the different foods that are added together to make a dish

LMNO

LADLE to use a deep spoon to transfer soups, stews or liquid

MARINATE or MARINATED food has been coated in a mixture of ingredients and left for a specific amount of time to add flavour

MIX to put the ingredients together and stir them well to combine

PQR

RINSE to hold the ingredient under running cold water to clean or cool quickly

ROUGH or ROUGHLY cut ingredients into small uneven size pieces

S

SEASON to add salt and pepper to enhance the flavour to taste

SIMMER to bubble gently just below boiling point, there should only be a few bubbles occasionally breaking the surface

SNIP or SNIPPED food that has been cut into small pieces using scissors

SOFTEN to change the texture of an ingredient to make them softer

STRIP to remove, for example remove the leaves from the basil stalk

TUV

TENDER the texture of the food after it has been lightly cooked. A wooden skewer should easily pierce through the food.

TRIM to remove the unwanted, damaged or inedible part of the food

WXYZ

ZEST the outer peel of a citrus fruit, used as flavouring

Look out for the next
Kookey Chefs book... and
don't forget to check out
our Kookey website and
facebook page!

www.facebook.com/thekookeychefs

www.thekookeychefs.co.uk